TANNER G

How to Keep a Budget

A Quick Start Budgeting Guide For Young Couples

This book was professionally typeset on Reedsy.
Find out more at reedsy.com

Contents

1 Introduction   1

2 The Bare Bones   3

3 Tracking Expenses   9

4 Your Financial Picture as a Whole   17

5 Setting Goals for the Future: Painting a Picture of Your...   21

6 Conclusion   30

7 Resources   37

1

Introduction

Welcome to a practical and purpose-driven guide to transforming your financial landscape. I'm excited you're here because this book is all about making budgeting work for you and your partner. No frills or complicated jargon—just straightforward advice to help you take control of your money and hopefully strengthen your relationship along the way.

Why did I write this book? Simple. I've been through the maze of managing finances with my wife, and I know it can be a bit overwhelming. This book is my way of sharing what I've learned, some of the successes, and the lessons, to make your journey smoother.

In the upcoming chapters, we'll break down budgeting into manageable steps. We'll start with tracking your expenses, move on to understanding your financial landscape, and then create a budget that suits your unique situation. But it's not just about the numbers; it's about building a stronger connection with your partner through shared financial goals.

This introduction sets the stage for the practical advice that follows. No need to be a financial guru—we're keeping it simple and useful. And here's a tip: make sure to check out the end of the book for example templates and tracking sheets that will help kick start your budgeting journey. Let's get started on this journey toward financial empowerment. Chapter 2 awaits, where we'll dive into the essential elements of effective budgeting. Here's to making your money work for you!

2

The Bare Bones

Welcome to the core of our financial mission – where we break down the essentials without the overwhelm. Let's dive into the bare bones of budgeting, ensuring you're armed with the knowledge to make informed decisions and stay on course.

What is Tracking Your Finances?

Tracking your finances is the cornerstone of financial empowerment, creating a detailed blueprint for your budget. It's where every financial move is documented, providing a comprehensive report of your monthly expenses. This isn't just about the big-ticket items like rent or mortgage payments; it's about capturing every financial nuance, from major expenditures to the seemingly trivial daily expenses. Yes, even that daily dose of caffeine or the occasional snack – because those seemingly small purchases have a tendency to add up swiftly.

Beyond just recording transactions, tracking allows you to visualize where your expenses are flowing and understand how they impact your overall financial landscape. It's like having a map that guides you through the terrain of your spending habits, helping you make informed decisions and stay on course.

What is Budgeting?

Budgeting acts as your financial compass, and tracking is the essential platform that puts it into action. Once you've diligently tracked your expenses, budgeting becomes the strategic tool to allocate your resources effectively. It's not about constraints but rather a road map guiding your money towards your priorities.

Here's a crucial insight: Many budgets fail not because of the concept but due to common pitfalls. One frequent misstep is setting unrealistic expectations, creating a budget that's too rigid and unattainable. Life is dynamic, and your budget should be adaptable, reflecting your ever-changing circumstances. Another stumbling block is neglecting to account for occasional expenses, like holidays or emergencies. Acknowledging these challenges and preparing strategies to overcome them will be one of your greatest challenges within your finances.

Become Unified in Your Desires to be Financially Free:

Starting a marriage or a partnership is undoubtedly a thrilling journey, but let's face it – it can be hard. My wife and I, like many others, struggled to even begin talking about finances. More often than not, what should have been simple conversations about money turned into tense silences or arguments before we could even address how we were handling our finances. The word "Money" quickly became a trigger, sparking emotions that made open dialogue challenging.

A midst the excitement in this new chapter of your life, be aware that one of the main stumbling blocks early on will likely revolve around money. Financial disagreements can strain even the most robust relationships. However, this section isn't about dwelling on challenges; it's about navigating them together and emerging stronger.

Understanding that financial unity is a cornerstone of a successful partnership, I hope that this book will serve as a guide to aligning your desires to be financially free. Communication is key, and we'll explore how to initiate those sometimes tricky conversations about money. It's not about pointing fingers but rather finding common ground and shared aspirations. Let's transform potential conflicts into opportunities for growth and solidarity.

Setting Realistic Expectations:

Embarking on the journey of setting financial goals as a couple is an exciting venture, but it's crucial to set realistic expectations from the start. Let's ponder a few questions together to guide your thinking:

Are we comfortable with the level of financial transparency we currently have, and how can we improve it?

- Open communication is key to financial unity. Assess your comfort levels with sharing financial details and explore ways to enhance transparency.*

What are our short-term and long-term financial goals as a couple?

- Consider immediate needs like paying off debts or saving for a vacation, as well as long-term goals such as buying a home or planning for retirement.

How do our individual spending habits align, and where might we need to compromise?

- Acknowledge and discuss any disparities in your spending habits. This conversation lays the groundwork for finding a middle ground that respects both your individual values and your shared financial goals.

Have we factored in unexpected expenses and emergencies in our budget?

- Life is unpredictable, and financial plans should account for the unexpected. Discuss how you'll handle unforeseen expenses without derailing your financial goals.

Have we considered individual financial goals within our shared financial vision?

- While working towards shared goals, it's essential to acknowledge and support each other's individual aspirations. Striking a balance ensures both personal fulfillment and collective success.

For new couples, it's common to overlook certain aspects or assume that financial alignment will happen naturally. The above questions aim to prompt discussions on these critical questions, fostering a deeper understanding of each other's financial expectations. We want to create a safe space where one of you isn't dragging the other along.

*I want to add a quick note here about transparency with each other. If you are going to live together, and start a life together... My recommendation is to go all in. There are plenty of people who make it work having two different bank accounts and more power to them! But if one of your goals is to become closer to each other, then merge bank accounts, share account numbers, credit cards, and give access to your spouse or partner. It will make these conversations SO much easier if everything is out in the open. There won't be a need to keep secrets and you are opening yourself up in such a way that will cement the financial foundation of your partnership. That said, whatever you choose will work as long as you are willing to make it work!

The Financial Goals WORTH Pursuing

As you embark on your journey towards financial freedom as a couple, it's crucial to outline clear and achievable goals. Let's break down these aspirations into three stages of life: short-term, midterm, and long-term financial goals.

Short-Term Financial Goals:

- Emergency Fund: Build a safety net to cover three to six months' worth of living expenses, providing financial security in unforeseen circumstances.
- Debt Repayment: Prioritize paying off high-interest debts, such as credit cards or personal loans, to reduce financial stress.
- Monthly Budgeting: Develop a comprehensive monthly budget that aligns with your financial priorities and helps control discretionary spending.

Mid-Term Financial Goals:

- Home ownership: Save for a down payment on a home, a significant milestone that provides stability and potential long-term financial growth.
- Education Fund: Invest in furthering education or skill development to enhance career prospects and earning potential.
- Investments: Begin building a diversified investment portfolio to grow wealth over time and prepare for long-term financial objectives.

Long-Term Financial Goals:

- Retirement Planning: Contribute regularly to retirement accounts, ensuring a comfortable and financially secure retirement.
- Children's Education: Save for your children's education expenses,

whether through a college fund or other educational savings plans.

- Estate Planning: Establish an estate plan, including wills and trusts, to protect your assets and ensure a smooth transfer of wealth to future generations.

Remember, these examples are starting points, and your financial goals should reflect your unique values and aspirations as a couple. The above goals are intended to inspire discussions and provide a road map for setting financial goals that align with your shared vision for the future. Not all financial goals are created equal. Explore the goals that truly matter to you as a unit, and as individuals, they are the ones that will shape your financial future. Also keep in mind that this is just the beginning! Keeping an open mind as you move forward can only be of benefit!

Lastly, be patient with each other. Create goals that allow both of you to win, don't give up your dreams, just change the path to the end goal to provide more opportunities to make each other's dreams reality. You will be surprised how quickly you find joy and excitement in making your partner's dream a priority.

3

Tracking Expenses

Why Budgets Fail: Unveiling the Common Pitfalls

As we navigate the complexities of tracking expenses, it's crucial to understand the stumbling blocks that often lead budgets astray. Our exploration begins with the recognition that unforeseen expenses and inflexibility are frequently the culprits behind budget failures, often catching us by surprise.

Unrealistic Expectations: A Foundation for Budget Failure:
While Chapter 2 emphasized the importance of setting achievable goals, the foundation for budget failure often lies in unrealistic expectations. This subsection revisits the notion of goal-setting, emphasizing the need for pragmatism in your financial aspirations. By aligning your goals with the realities of your life, you create a sturdy platform for successful budgeting.

Unforeseen Expenses: The Stealthy Adversaries of Budgets:
Unforeseen expenses have a knack for catching us off guard. This section explores the nature of these unexpected costs and provides

strategies for anticipating and mitigating their impact on your budget. By acknowledging the inevitability of surprises, you can better fortify your financial plan against their stealthy intrusion.

Inflexibility: A Rigidity That Breeds Discontent:
Inflexibility is another common saboteur of budgets. As life unfolds, circumstances change, and a budget that can't adapt becomes a source of frustration. We'll delve into the importance of building flexibility into your financial plan, allowing you to navigate the twists and turns of life without sacrificing your financial goals.

By addressing these common pitfalls, we pave the way for a budget that is not only about tracking expenses but also about creating a dynamic, adaptable financial plan.

The Tracking Process: A Month of Financial Discovery
Before we dive into the intricacies of budgeting, let's illuminate the transformative process of tracking expenses. Imagine it as a month-long voyage of financial discovery, where you become intimately acquainted with your spending habits, patterns, and financial landscape.

- Initiating the Tracking Journey:
- Begin by noting every expense, regardless of size, in a dedicated tracking journal or a digital tool. From significant purchases to the seemingly trivial, capture them all. This is the raw data that will unveil your financial story.

Here is an example of a basic way to track your expenses (Using Google Sheets is a great way to get a lot of data and easily share between you and your significant other):

	A	B	C	D	E
1	Date	Item	Price	Type	Total
2					
3					
4					
5					
6					
7					
8					
9					
10					
11					

Regardless of how you set it up, having the date is key. It will allow you to start creating a habit and you will easily be able to pick up where you left off.

The item column is a super basic example of what your purchase was. If you went to fill up your car, name the item gas. If you went to Starbucks and bought yourself an Iced Tea then call it Starbucks. Etc. If needed, add some notes to help you remember what you were purchasing. As you spend more time tracking you will find that it isn't as critical to know the exact details as you might think.

Price should be pretty straight forward, so include it! You can either keep your receipts or find them later when looking through transactions on your credit or debit cards. Whatever is easiest for you.

Type may be a little more confusing. This is how we differentiate the different accounts that our money is coming from. I do this because we have a couple different credit cards, and two different checking accounts. Though there could be an entire chapter on this philosophy I will be brief by saying, using credit cards when you can maximize benefits can be extremely fruitful. If you have debts and struggle to stay on top of a credit card I wouldn't recommend this practice and I would instead think, "when could I have used my debit card instead of my credit card to avoid piling up more debt?" - This is also the location I like to add notes if I have any.

And finally, you want to see how much you have spent over the course of the month! So in the cell underneath "Total" type in the following:

=sum(C:C)

"C" represents the column where you are adding all your prices, and that nifty equation will save you time by adding up all your expenses for you!

If you are doing this budget by hand! I salute you, I hope you have a calculator!

This is how you will successfully track money that is leaving your financial storage! You may ask, "What about the money that I am making?"

Great question! Typically that comes in far less often and is relatively straight forward. Here is a recommended template that I built:

In whichever order you would like I would recommend having the following in place,

Income, a tab to track how much money is coming in. This can be built similar to the price of your expenses.

INCOME	Type	Total	Month End

Type, similar to the above here is where you mark what it is, not critical, but makes it easier if you have a lot going on! (My income versus my wife's income)

Total will be the sum of all your income (=sum(here just grab the cells you are using))

Lastly, I recommend having a Month's End. By inserting the following equation you will be able to see whether your finances are headed in a positive or a negative direction.

   (=sum(*the cell that holds the sum of your income minus (-) the cell under total within your spending section)

I hope the following diagram will make the above more clear:

E	F	G	H	I
Total	INCOME	Type	Total	Month End
				? =sum(H2-E2

From here all you have to do is keep track of all money movements and you will have the road map you need to help determine your budget!

Before moving on to how to budget, I want to add a few thoughts for you and yours to think about.

- Regular Check-Ins:
- Regularly review your tracking data throughout the month. This ongoing assessment allows you to stay aware of your spending trends and enables real-time adjustments.
- Reflecting on Patterns:
- As the month unfolds, patterns will emerge. Identify areas where you consistently spend more or areas where you could potentially cut back. This reflection is a powerful tool for informed decision-making.
- Diagnosing Spending Habits:
- By the end of the month, you'll have a comprehensive view of your spending habits. Are you an impulse buyer? Do certain situations trigger specific expenses? This diagnosis sets the stage for intentional and mindful spending.
- Categorizing Expenditures:
- Create categories that align with your lifestyle. Housing, transportation, groceries, entertainment – tailor them to fit your unique circumstances. Categorization provides a clearer snapshot of where

your money is flowing. (This will be far more applicable to your budget but is important to start thinking about now)

A couple of notes.

Getting into the Habit of Tracking Your Expenses

Tracking your expenses is not just about recording transactions; it's a mindset shift that forms the foundation of financial control. This section is a guide to help cultivate the habit of tracking, making it a seamless part of your daily routine. By adopting a proactive approach to monitoring your spending, you'll gain valuable insights into your financial habits, paving the way for informed decision-making

Envision this tracking process as a standalone phase before budgeting. It's an invitation to immerse yourself in a month of financial self-discovery. Allow this process to unfold before crafting your budget, and you'll be equipped with the insights needed to shape a financial plan that aligns with your values and aspirations.

Time: A Lifelong Commitment to Financial Growth or Not

Time is a powerful factor in financial success. I hope this section allows you to explore the concept of long-term financial growth and the impact of small, consistent efforts over time. By embracing the idea of financial growth as a lifelong commitment, you'll be better equipped to weather economic changes, navigate various life stages, and achieve lasting financial stability.

If you decide that this takes too much time, don't bother reading any further, take a couple of hours of your day and track your expenses for LAST month. That will allow you to immediately see everything you have previously done and your habits won't have had time to change since you likely weren't thinking about budgeting until now! Once that is done, have a conversation about creating categories and get into the next chapter!

Lastly, If you are anything like me, and data fascinates you, you may find yourself going back months and compiling ALL of your spending since the beginning! I cannot promise that more data will actually help you. Let's remember that today marks the day you changed your future, not your past.

4

Your Financial Picture as a Whole

IF YOU DO NOT HAVE A MONTHS WORTH OF TRACKING THIS CHAPTER IS WORTHLESS.

If you have done the tracking, you are now armed with a month's worth of meticulously tracked expenses. It's time to sit down and assess your current financial landscape and strategically plan for the future.

Based on What You Have Tracked: Where Are You Now?

Reflect on the patterns and insights gathered from your tracking journey. This section prompts you to assess your current financial standing. Are there areas where you've overspent or perhaps surprised yourself with disciplined savings? Understanding where you are now provides a baseline for setting realistic and achievable goals.

Here I invite you to sit as a couple and complete a few exercises.

Vocalize where you think YOU have overspent! This is not the time to point out each other's flaws. If you do, you will kill your budget! I was a major savor in our relationship. I really didn't spend much day to day. That said when I did decide to spend money it typically wasn't a small spend! My wife usually had far smaller spends but they were daily! No amount of me pointing out to her that her daily spends added up would have changed a thing! But when we implemented this change and we saw collectively that my spends were far too big, and her spends significantly added up over time we were able to come to an agreement that gave us all the freedom we needed but also allowed us to strategically spend our money.

After you have each shared your personal overspending let's make sure you start getting things into different categories. I will share what I use in addition to some categories that I think I will use in the future, it may or may not be useful. If it isn't, hopefully it gives you something to build off of.

- Rent or mortgage
- Car Payment
- Investments - This could be Money Markets, IRA's, Stocks. (I am not including company matches here or what I might put into a retirement account if the company I work for offers such a thing)
- Donations - not typical for young couples, but is a constant in our relationship, I firmly believe that the more I give, the more I get. (within reason)
- Insurance - Rental, Home, Health, Car, Life, etc. It all goes here.
- Phone Bill - Typically the same every month unless you are paying by the minute
- WIFI
- Vacation - this is an interesting one. It is used both as a method to save for future savings and for the money spent during the month on out of the ordinary travel.

- House Maintenance
- Car Maintenance
- Gifts
- Medical
- Groceries - We typically include things like hygiene and clothing within this category we quickly found that the more strict we were, the harder on both of us.
- Gas - Vehicles
- Bills - Gas, Electricity, Water, and Waste Management. (I actually like to split these into their respective categories since they change month to month)
- Restaurant - Any time you go out to eat
- Dates
- Me
- My Spouse
- Entertainment - Subscriptions here like music or TV.

Use your spending to build out these categories, what I have above isn't for everyone and I do want to add once more that you need to be flexible, the more rigid you are the harder it gets. Also be fair to each other! If you go with my categories, it isn't a freebie to spend $500 on clothes and then add it to groceries. If all the clothes are yours, put it under yourself! You will know how it will work best as you have this conversation.

If you come across something that genuinely doesn't fit into any of the categories you have selected, but it doesn't make sense to have a category for something that hardly ever occurs, I advise creating an "other" or "miscellaneous" category! Use it sparingly.

Additionally, it is important to remember that although you are working together, there should be space for your individuality. The goal of a budget isn't to create a robotic lifestyle, rather promote excitement and joy within reason! Having some spare money for your own personal discretion will help you fight through the sometimes difficult days of adulting! Since it is personal and limited it should also help prevent future arguments about overspending or increase conversation revolving around why you are overspending.

Once you are done with the above it is time for the most difficult part of this entire mission! Putting realistic numbers to your budget!

5

Setting Goals for the Future: Painting a Picture of Your Priorities

Envision your financial future by setting clear and purposeful goals. What are your short-term and long-term aspirations? I encourage you to paint a vivid picture of your priorities. Whether it's debt reduction, saving for a home, or planning for a comfortable retirement, let your goals guide the direction of where you limit your spending and where you give more for your spending. To help with this I have created a guide to give you a more general view of what your categories from chapter 4 actually are.

A few definitions to keep in mind.

- *Fixed Income:* Establish a clear understanding of your stable, recurring income sources. This forms the bedrock of your budget, providing financial stability. Your overall spending should not exceed this number unless in dire circumstances.
- *Variable Needs and Wants:* Distinguish between essential, fluctuating expenses (needs) and discretionary spending (wants). This differentiation lays the groundwork for intentional allocation.
- *Future Needs and Wants:* Identify savings goals for upcoming

necessities and aspirational wants. These categories ensure you're not just living in the present but actively preparing for the future. Although it might feel constrictive, this is where the fun happens. By saving a little bit now you will be able to save yourself from the heartache that debt can create and add to more meaningful experiences as you achieve your financial goals to go on dream vacations, pay off debt, and become financially free!

These ideas create a space for your subcategories, or the categories that you created in chapter 4.

- *Fixed Expenses:* Within this category, consider subcategories like housing, utilities, insurance, and loan repayments. This detailed breakdown adds precision to your budgeting process.
- *Variable Needs:* Subdivide into groceries, transportation, and bills. This granularity enhances your ability to track and control variable expenses.
- *Variable Wants:* Explore subcategories such as dining out, entertainment, and personal indulgences. This segmentation allows for conscious spending on discretionary items.
- *Future Needs and Wants:* Break down savings goals into subcategories, whether it's for education, a home, future medical bills, or a vacation. This step ensures you're allocating funds strategically towards your future priorities.

Here is an example of what this would look like in a personalized budget using many of the categories expressed above.

FIXED	Rent/Mortgage
	Car Payment
	Investments
	Donations
	Insurance
	Phone Bill
	WIFI
Future Needs	Vacation
	House Maintenance
	Car Maintenance
	Gifts
	Medical
Variable Needs	Groceries
	Gas
	Bills
	Restaurant
Variable Wants	Dates
	You
	Your Spouse
	Entertainment
	Other

You may have heard of the concept of paying yourself first, we are going to follow that advice as we plan out what your budget is going to look like. We are going to break this down piece by piece starting with "Fixed", or fixed expenses. Your fixed expenses are the monthly payments that do not change in amount (unless you move, or have a drastic lifestyle change). These are the first things that come out of your monthly income.

So as a quick example, for your fixed expenses let's say you pay rent of $1500, you have a car payment of $425, your phone bill is $75 and your WiFi is $50. So without fail you are guaranteed to spend $2050 per month. None of the above expenses will change on you without some sort of warning.

Future Needs are the second part of paying yourself first. Every month you want to do what you can to put some amount into savings. Even if it is basic. To help with that we budget for specific expenses we know will come down the road. If you own a house there will come a day when something breaks, an AC unit, the furnace, or you may find yourself replacing your roof. Car ownership is no less expensive, in addition to the frequent expenses like oil changes, filter changes, windshield wipers, tire rotations, and the fuel to operate, you may find yourself with a big fix, like a timing belt gone bad, or the transmission going out. These expenses will come and you will want to put some money aside each month to help when that time comes. You know your house and vehicle(s) better than I do, you will know how much to set aside. For us it has been a learning curve. We are still working on finding the right amount but that is the great thing about this type of budgeting! It is built to last as long as you put the time into it!

Variable Needs and Wants are pretty self explanatory, but once you have added up your expenses from your month of tracking into each category you will be able to get an idea of how much you spend per month per category, however you build your budget I recommend having a space to add everything up, I will include the numbers from our above example to help clarify the system I suggest.

See below.

		Monthly Spending	Budget
FIXED	Rent/Mortgage	$1,500.00	$1,500.00
	Car Payment	$425.00	$425.00
	Investments		
	Donations		
	Insurance		
	Phone Bill	$75.00	$75.00
	WIFI	$50.00	$50.00
Future Needs	Vacation		
	House Maintenance		
	Car Maintenance		
	Gifts		
	Medical		
Variable Needs	Groceries		
	Gas		
	Bills		
	Restaurant		
Variable Wants	Dates		
	You		
	Your Spouse		
	Entertainment		
	Other		
	Total	=SUM(P7:P27)	=SUM(Q7:Q27)

I am also going to share an example that is close to what my wife and I tracked for the first month of our marriage. We were still working on getting everything in our names and luckily we had extremely supportive parents who were very patient with us as we were transitioning.

Using this example hopefully I can explain the thought process behind why we created the budget we did.

		Monthly Spending	Budget
FIXED	Rent/Mortgage	$675.00	$675.00
	Car Payment	$270.00	$270.00
	Investments	$40.00	$40.00
	Donations		
	Insurance		
	Phone Bill		
	WIFI		
Future Needs	Vacation	$60.00	$100.00
	House Maintenance		
	Car Maintenance		
	Gifts	$400.00	$50.00
	Medical		
Variable Needs	Groceries	$230.00	$240.00
	Gas	$200.00	$250.00
	Bills(Utilities)	$250.00	$300.00
	Restaurant	$160.00	$100.00
Variable Wants	Dates		
	You	$50.00	$15.00
	Your Spouse	$75.00	$15.00
	Entertainment	$5.00	$10.00
	Other	$230.00	
	Total	$2,645.00	$2,065.00

Now when my wife and I looked at our spending there were a few things that quickly caught our eye. Our spending was far more than we expected it to be. Look at our gift section specifically. I couldn't tell you how we spent nearly half of what we spent on our apartment over the course of the month on gifts. We determined that we could still give each other, and others, gifts but it would need a serious check. So we decided that $50 a month or $600 a year would be sufficient. For a while it was. That has changed since then as we have started making more each month and as our families have gotten bigger.

Something else I want to bring to your attention is the "other" category. At the beginning we weren't sure where to put expenditures that my wife was making for work that would later be reimbursed. Clothes had a category which isn't shown. Plenty of expenditures that just didn't fit. That other category began to dwindle as we created a budget that matched our lifestyle.

Lastly, note where we limited our spending the most? We limited our own personal spending in a big way! $15 a month is not much to work with. Our priority at that time was spending time with each other and that meant going out to eat. You will also notice that I haven't explained why the restaurant category falls under a "Need" rather than a "Want". That developed from a conversation with my wife, at the time there were days when neither one of us had time to make dinner. Eating is a need in order to live and therefore some of our finances would be allotted to filling that need when the circumstance presented itself. It was that same principle that later led to us creating a "Date" category. We cut some of the budget for our needed restaurants and added to the date budget. It fell under "Wants" and added to the ever growing budget system that fit our exact hopes and strategies for planning our finances in a meaningful way.

So, what now? Using your Tracking, begin to divide up your budget categories, leverage the insights gained from your tracking journey to allocate funds within each category. This personalized approach ensures that your budget reflects your lifestyle and values. Ensure your budget is realistic and attainable. As has been mentioned, by setting achievable goals, you create opportunities for early wins. This positive reinforcement is crucial for sustaining long-term financial discipline.

Use Your Budget and Make Adjustments Accordingly

Your budget is a dynamic tool, not a rigid plan. Regularly assess and adjust based on changing circumstances and goals. This adaptability ensures that your budget remains a guiding force throughout various stages of your financial journey.

I hope that using this pivotal section, you have transformed your financial vision into a tangible budget, breaking down key categories and guiding you towards intentional spending. I can honestly say that budgeting was one of the best things that ever happened to my wife and I's relationship. Our conversations about money, which were plagued with tears and conflict have evaporated. Our conversations now are how to grow and prepare for the next step. It has been a long process and I can't say that I have reached financial freedom yet. The day is coming and I hope that you will be able to say the same thing as you implement this.

6

Conclusion

Congratulations on completing this transformative journey toward financial empowerment! In the pages of this book, you've explored the intricacies of tracking expenses, setting realistic goals, and crafting a budget that aligns with your unique values and aspirations.

As you reflect on the insights gained, remember that financial success is not about restriction but rather intentional and mindful choices. By tracking your expenses, you've unveiled the patterns that shape your financial landscape. Setting goals has given you a road map, and your budget is the tool that turns those aspirations into reality.

The journey doesn't end here; it's a continuous evolution. Embrace the flexibility of your budget, making adjustments as life unfolds and your priorities shift. Cultivate a positive mindset toward money, recognizing it as a tool for enhancing your life rather than a source of stress.

Financial empowerment is a journey that requires commitment, adaptability, and a proactive approach to your financial well-being. By implementing the principles and strategies outlined in this book, you've laid the foundation for a lifetime of financial success.

There are plenty of things that were not mentioned within this book. Debt management, how to make more money, where to put my investments. That may come down the road. But for now I can't say that I have the experience I want to be able to successfully write something for you that will prove useful. If you struggle with debt, use this book to magnify your savings towards bringing that down. If you are saving a ton already, then consider meeting with a financial advisor. They are often free for the first meeting!

Now, if you found this helpful please share your thoughts and experiences by leaving a review on Amazon. Your feedback not only helps others considering this journey but also contributes to a community of individuals committed to financial empowerment.

Thank you for allowing this book to be a part of your journey. May your financial future be filled with prosperity, security, and the fulfillment of your dreams.

And as promised I wanted to make sure you had access to a month's worth of tracking and a quick-start budget. Enjoy in whatever form works best for you!

	Date	Item	Price	Type
	1/1/2000	Rent (example)		Checking
Week 1				

	Date	Item	Price	Type
Week 2				

	Date	Item	Price	Type
Week 3				

	Date	Item	Price	Type
Week 4				

Total (add all expenses here)	INCOME	Type	Total Income	Month End (Total Income - Total Expenses)

		Monthly Spending	Budget
FIXED	Rent/Mortgage		
	Car Payment		
	Investments		
	Donations		
	Insurance		
	Phone Bill		
	WIFI		
Future Needs	Vacation		
	House Maintenance		
	Car Maintenance		
	Gifts		
	Medical		
Variable Needs	Groceries		
	Gas		
	Bills(Utilities)		
	Restaurant		
Variable Wants	Dates		
	You		
	Your Spouse		
	Entertainment		
	Other		
	Total		

Typically color-coordinating your expenditures and this picture will help you add up your monthly spending

7

Resources

OpenAI. (2024). ChatGPT (Version 3.5). OpenAI. https://chat.openai.c om/